READ & RESPOND

Helping children discover the pleasure and p

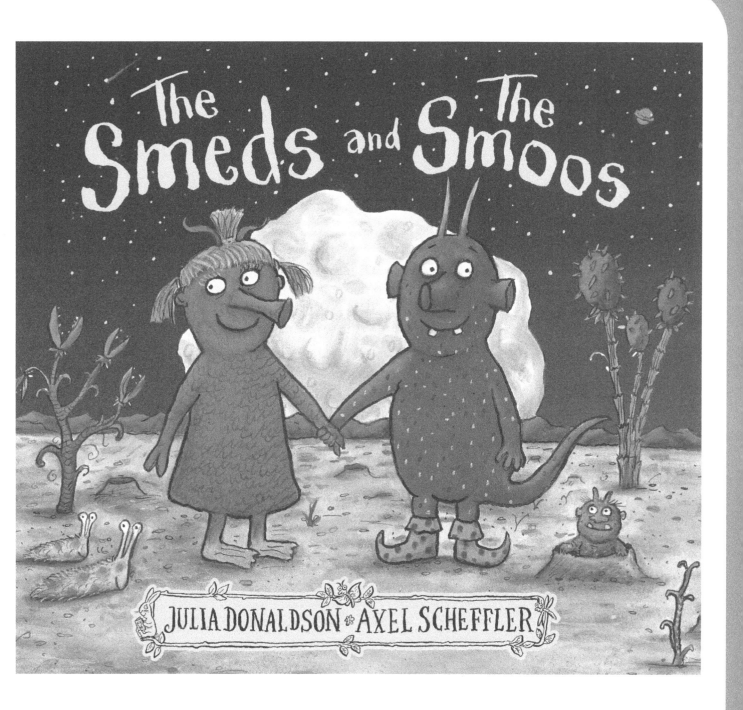

The Smeds and The Smoos

JULIA DONALDSON • AXEL SCHEFFLER

FOR AGES 5–7

Published in the UK by Scholastic, 2022

Scholastic Distribution Centre, Bosworth Avenue, Tournament Fields, Warwick, CV34 6UQ

Scholastic Ireland, 89E Lagan Road, Dublin Industrial Estate, Glasnevin, Dublin, D11 HP5F

SCHOLASTIC and associated logos are trademarks and/or registered trademarks of Scholastic Inc.

www.scholastic.co.uk

© 2022 Scholastic Limited

1 2 3 4 5 6 7 8 9   2 3 4 5 6 7 8 9 0 1

A CIP catalogue record for this book is available from the British Library.
ISBN 978-0702-31948-8

Printed and bound by Ashford Colour Press

The book is made of materials from well-managed,
FSC®-certified forests and other controlled sources.

Extracts from *The National Curriculum in England, English Programme of Study* © Crown Copyright. Reproduced under the terms of the Open Government Licence (OGL). http://www.nationalarchives.gov.uk/doc/open-government-licence/version/3

Author Samantha Pope

Editorial team Rachel Morgan, Vicki Yates, Suzanne Adams, Caroline Hale

Series designer Andrea Lewis

Typesetter QBS Learning

Illustrator Emiliano Migliardo

Acknowledgements

The publishers gratefully acknowledge permission to reproduce the following copyright material: **Scholastic UK** for the use of the Extract and illustrations from *The Smeds and The Smoos* by Julia Donaldson and Axel Scheffler, text copyright © 2019 Julia Donaldson, illustrations copyright © Axel Scheffler (2019, Alison Green Books).

Every effort has been made to trace copyright holders for the works reproduced in this book, and the publishers apologise for any inadvertent omissions.

For supporting online resources go to:
www.scholastic.co.uk/read-and-respond/books/the-smeds-and-the-smoos/online-resources
Access key: With

CONTENTS ▼

How to use Read & Respond in your classroom...

Read & Respond provides teaching ideas related to a specific well-loved children's book. Each Read & Respond book is divided into the following sections:

ABOUT THE BOOK AND AUTHOR

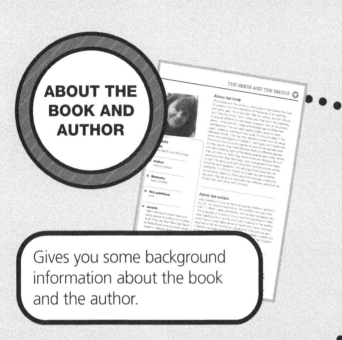

Gives you some background information about the book and the author.

GUIDED READING

Breaks the book down into sections and gives notes for using it, ideal for use with the whole class. A bookmark has been provided on page 10 containing **comprehension** questions. The children can be directed to refer to these as they read. Find comprehensive guided reading sessions on he supporting online resources.

SHARED READING

Provides extracts from the children's book with associated notes for focused work. There is also one non-fiction extract that relates to the children's book.

PHONICS & SPELLING

Provides word-level work related to the children's book so you can teach phonics, spelling and **vocabulary** in context.

PLOT, CHARACTER & SETTING

Contains activity ideas focused on the plot, characters and the setting of the story.

TALK ABOUT IT

Oracy, **fluency**, and speaking and listening activities. These activities may be based directly on the children's book or be broadly based on the themes and concepts of the story.

GET WRITING

Provides writing activities related to the children's book. These activities may be based directly on the children's book or be broadly based on the themes and concepts of the story.

ASSESSMENT

Contains short activities that will help you assess whether the children have understood concepts and curriculum objectives. They are designed to be informal activities to feed into your planning.

SUPPORTING ONLINE RESOURCE

Online you can find a host of supporting documents including planning information, comprehensive guided reading sessions and guidance on teaching reading.

www.scholastic.co.uk/read-and-respond/books/
the-smeds-and-the-smoos/online-resources
Access key: With

Help children develop a love of reading for pleasure.

Activities

The activities follow the same format:

- **Objective:** the objective for the lesson. It will be based upon a curriculum objective, but will often be more specific to the focus being covered.

- **What you need:** a list of resources you need to teach the lesson, including photocopiable pages.

- **What to do:** the activity notes.

- **Differentiation:** this is provided where specific and useful differentiation advice can be given to support and/or extend the learning in the activity. Differentiation by providing additional adult support has not been included as this will be at a teacher's discretion based upon specific children's needs and ability, as well as the availability of support.

The activities are numbered for reference within each section and should move through the text sequentially – so you can use the lesson while you are reading the book. Once you have read the book, most of the activities can be used in any order you wish.

CURRICULUM LINKS

Section	Activity	Curriculum objectives
Guided reading		Comprehension: To participate in discussion about what is read to them; to explain clearly their understanding of what is read to them.
Shared reading	1	Comprehension: To draw on what they already know or on background information and vocabulary provided by the teacher.
	2	Comprehension: To discuss and clarify word meanings, linking new meanings to known vocabulary.
	3	Comprehension: To listen to and discuss a wide range of poetry, stories and non-fiction.
Phonics & spelling	1	Spelling: To use the spelling rule for adding '-s' or '-es' as the plural marker for nouns.
	2	Word reading: To read words with contractions (for example, I'm, I'll, we'll) and understand that the apostrophe represents the omitted letter(s).
	3	Spoken language: To use relevant strategies to build their vocabulary.
	4	Spelling: To use '-ed' where no change is needed in the spelling of the root words.
Plot, character & setting	1	Comprehension: To link what they read or hear read to their own experiences.
	2	Comprehension: To discuss the sequence of events.
	3	Comprehension: To participate in discussion about books…read to them, taking turns and listening to what others say.
	4	Comprehension: To make inferences on the basis of what is being said and done.
	5	Comprehension: To listen to and discuss a wide range of poems at a level beyond that at which they can read independently.
	6	Spoken language: To articulate and justify answers, arguments and opinions.
Talk about it	1	Spoken language: To listen and respond appropriately to adults and their peers.
	2	Spoken language: To give well-structured descriptions, explanations and narratives for different purposes.
	3	Spoken language: To participate in role play and improvisations.
	4	Spoken language: To consider and evaluate different viewpoints, attending to and building on the contributions of others.
	5	Spoken language: To speak audibly and fluently.
	6	Spoken language: To ask relevant questions to extend their understanding and knowledge.
Get writing	1	Composition: To discuss what they have written with the teacher or other pupils.
	2	Vocabulary, grammar and punctuation: To begin to punctuate sentences using a capital letter and a full stop, question mark or exclamation mark.
	3	Composition: To sequence sentences to form short narratives.
	4	Composition: To read aloud their writing clearly enough to be heard by their peers and the teacher.
	5	Composition: To say out loud what they are going to write about.
	6	Spelling: To spell the days of the week.
Assessment	1	Vocabulary, grammar and punctuation: To learn how to use expanded noun phrases to describe and specify.
	2	Spoken language: To use spoken language to develop understanding through speculating, hypothesising, imagining and exploring ideas.
	3	Vocabulary, grammar and punctuation: To develop their understanding of the concepts set out in English Appendix 2 by joining words and clauses using 'and'.
	4	Composition: To develop positive attitudes towards writing by writing for different purposes.

Key facts

◉ **Title:**
The Smeds and The Smoos

◉ **Author:**
Julia Donaldson

◉ **Illustrator:**
Axel Scheffler

◉ **First published:**
2019

◉ **Awards:**
Julia's and Axel's books have won many awards including the Smarties Book Prize, the Blue Peter Best Book to Read Aloud, and the British Book Awards Children's Book of the Year.

◉ **Did you know?**
In 2019, the Royal Mail commissioned special stamps to celebrate the 20th birthday of *The Gruffalo*.

About the book

The Smeds and The Smoos is a story poem that tackles the issue of prejudice and the importance of friendship in an inspiring and joyful way. The Smeds don't like the Smoos, and the Smoos don't like the Smeds. Why? Simply put, they don't like anything or anyone different to themselves. However, two of the young aliens – Janet and Bill – begin a friendship that horrifies their grandparents. The two rebel against orders never to meet again, creeping, 'whenever they could,/To sing and play in the Wurpular Wood.' One day they 'decided to wed' and ran away when their grandparents forbade it. Distraught, the Smeds and the Smoos have to work together to look for the beloved pair. As they search, they meet different aliens on different planets and start showing signs of friendship towards each other. When they can look no more, they return home and discover Bill and Janet and their 'dear little baby', who 'was purple, from head to toe!' The story ends with the Smeds and the Smoos united, full of joy and happiness. The last page in the book has the dedication 'To All the Children of Europe' by Axel Scheffler, encouraging readers to think about the message underlying the story: that we are all more alike than different, and that we should treat each other with kindness.

About the author

Julia Donaldson is one of the most popular children's authors in the UK. Her breakthrough book, *The Gruffalo*, has sold more than 17 million copies worldwide, and has been translated into 105 languages and dialects since it was first published in 1999. Julia's background in drama and music is obvious in her writing which has an undeniable sense of rhythm and rhyme. She was awarded a CBE for Services to Literature in 2019 and was also Children's Laureate from 2011 to 2013. Her website contains lots of fascinating information on her work and that of her frequent collaborator Axel Scheffler.

About the illustrator

German-born Axel Scheffler is an award-winning illustrator, perhaps best known for his partnership with Julia Donaldson. Together, they have published more than 22 books including the hugely popular *The Gruffalo, Stick Man, The Snail and the Whale, The Highway Rat* and *Zog*. Axel Scheffler has also worked with other writers and has written and illustrated many of his own books, too. He has illustrated over 100 books to date and won the inaugural Illustrator of the Year Award at the British Book Awards (the Nibbies) in 2018.

GUIDED READING ▶

Front and back covers

Together, as a class, look at the front and back covers of the book before you start reading the story. Draw the children's attention to both the words and the illustrations. Just from the cover, can the children tell you what type of 'being' the Smeds and the Smoos are? (possibly aliens from another planet) Ask question 1 on the bookmark. Discuss together what the title suggests. (There are two groups of beings – one is known as the Smeds and the other as the Smoos. Their names are different, but they begin and end with the same letters, so this might suggest that they have more in common than they think.)

Ensure the children know what an author and an illustrator are. They may recognise Axel Scheffler's illustrative style, so confirm he is the illustrator and Julia Donaldson writes the words. Ask: *Can you think of any other books by the pair? If so, can you guess what this book will be like?*

Getting the most from the book

As you read through the book together, pay special attention to expression, particularly when reading the grandparents' speeches. Invite and involve the children in these parts – they will enjoy the repetition of 'Never, never'. Have fun with the nonsense words, such as 'loobular', 'humplety' and so on. Ask the children question 6 on the bookmark. (Examples of more 'normal' words: 'Loobular' could mean 'warm' and 'humplety' could be 'round'.) Enjoy the strange sounds created by the words, highlighting any alliteration or assonance, and see how they contribute to the rhythm. Pause where punctuation, such as ellipses and dashes, adds effect. Explain how the use of these adds to the book's suspense.

Spreads 1 to 3

Explain, as you read through the first few spreads, that these pages establish the scene, setting, characters and what the book is about. Define any of these words if the children are unsure of their meaning. Ask: *What is the author trying to tell us about the Smeds and the Smoos and their relationship to each other?* (They are different and they don't like each other.) *How are Janet and Bill different to the others?* Ask the children question 3 on the bookmark. Discuss how Bill and Janet are likely to be the most important characters in the story. Look together at the expressions on Janet's and Bill's faces compared to their friends' expressions. Ask question 8 on the bookmark. Discuss what could have led to the Smeds and the Smoos disliking each other. (For example, perhaps Grandfather Smed and Grandmother Smoo had a bad argument and this is why they are the ones who tell Janet and Bill to stay away from each other.)

Spreads 4 and 5

Spend some time looking at spread 4, where Bill and Janet meet in the Wurpular Wood. Ask: *How do Janet and Bill show friendship towards each other?* (smile, rub antennae, play, tell story and sing song, climb together) Next, contrast this with Grandfather Smed's and Grandmother Smoo's reactions when they find them together (spread 5). Highlight the adjectives 'nasty' and 'dreadful' and ask the children if these are nice things to say about someone. Ask: *How do you think Bill and Janet feel when they hear this and are told not to play together? Do Janet and Bill believe what their grandparents say?* Point out the expression: 'spoke her mind' and explain that this means Grandmother Smoo said exactly what she was thinking (even though it was unkind). Have the children ever 'spoken their mind' before? How did it make them – and the other person – feel?

Spreads 6 to 8

On spread 6, point out that Janet and Bill still meet each other. Ask: *Do you think Bill and Janet ever worry about being caught?* Look at the right-hand page, where Bill and Janet are told they cannot marry each other. Point out that this is the third time Grandfather Smed and Grandmother Smoo have said why Bill and Janet are not allowed to be friends. Ask the children question 4 on the bookmark. Explore the reasons the grandparents give, such as differences in where they sleep and what they eat and drink. Discuss how we all have different things we like and dislike but that doesn't mean we cannot be friends. Ask the children to justify their answers.

Next, look at spread 7 where Janet and Bill run away. Explore if the children think it is a good idea or not and whether they think Janet and Bill will return. Ask: *Do you think that it is all right for Janet and Bill to steal the Smeds' rocket, even if* 'Grandfather Smed had forgotten to lock it'*? Does the situation justify the act?* Next, look at spread 8 where the Smeds and the Smoos have discovered that Bill and Janet have gone. Encourage the children to look at the illustrations as well as the words before telling you how the Smeds and the Smoos must be feeling (worried, scared, panicked and surprised). When the Smeds and the Smoos agree to look for Bill and Janet together, ask if the children can explain why. Ask: *Have you ever had to work together to achieve something? What was it and was it better working with others?*

Spreads 9 to 12

These spreads look at the journey the Smoos and the Smeds take to find Janet and Bill. Look at the names of the planets together and enjoy their strange sounds: 'Vumjum', 'Lurglestrop', 'Grimbletosh', 'Glurch', 'Scloop' and 'Klaboo'. Then, ask the children question 5 on the bookmark. Explore how the Smeds' and the Smoos' exposure to so many different places and beings helps them to realise that differences between groups of beings is not a bad thing. Ask: *Does this affect the way the Smeds and the Smoos think about each other?* Look in particular at spread 11. Ask: *How are the Smeds and the Smoos acting towards each other here?* (They are beginning to share, mixing together and

helping each other.) Finally, see if any of the children have ever travelled to different countries, or even to different cities or places within their home country. Ask: *Does it matter to them if people aren't the same and eat different things?*

Spreads 13 to 15

The Smeds and the Smoos arrive home and find Bill and Janet. Ask the children to suggest how long the pair have been away and how they might have felt when they returned and no one was there. Show the children Spreads 13 and 14 and ask them question 9 on the bookmark. Compare these pages with the illustrations at the beginning and explore how the Smeds and the Smoos have changed in the book. (At the beginning, apart from Bill and Janet, the other Smoos always look worried or suspicious. At the end, they are all having fun and playing with each other.) Julia Donaldson repeats her earlier description of the Wurpular Wood: 'Where the trockles grew tall and the glompoms smelled good'. Explore together why she has done this (to show that all the Smeds and the Smoos now experience the wood in the same way as Janet and Bill in the beginning – with happiness). We meet the baby on spread 14 – ask the children question 2 on the bookmark. Discuss how the Smoo-Smed baby is purple because blue and red mixed together makes purple. Look at the baby and comment on how he is a mix of Bill and Janet. Ask: *Can you think of a better or different name for him?*

The mood at the end of the book is very different to the beginning, particularly on spread 14. Ask the children question 7 on the bookmark. (Words that show their happiness include: 'hugged', 'laughed', 'splashed', 'danced', 'delight', 'played'.) On the final spread, we have a new verse in italics. Compare it to the first verses earlier in the book which often begin with 'Never'. Ask: *How is this verse different?* Finally, ask the children question 10 on the bookmark and explore how the story is similar or different to what they expected. (Answers will differ here but might include that they thought the book would just be about the two characters on the front and they didn't know that they weren't allowed, at the beginning, to be friends.)

The Smeds and The Smoos
by Julia Donaldson & Axel Scheffler

Focus on... Meaning

1. Why is the book called *The Smeds and The Smoos* and not something else?
2. Why is Janet and Bill's baby purple and why is this important?

Focus on... Organisation

3. Why do you think we meet Janet and Bill on the very first pages and why do they have ordinary names?
4. Do you think the reasons why the Smeds and the Smoos dislike each other are good ones?
5. Why do you think we see the Smeds and the Smoos visiting so many different planets and meeting other aliens?

The Smeds and The Smoos
by Julia Donaldson & Axel Scheffler

Focus on... Language and features

6. There are lots of nonsense words in the book. Can you think of a real word to replace each one?
7. When the Smeds and the Smoos meet the baby, everyone is happy. Can you find words to show this?

Focus on... Purpose, viewpoints and effects

8. What do you think happened in the past to make the Smeds and the Smoos dislike each other?
9. Look at how the illustrator has drawn the Smeds and the Smoos at the end of the book. How do they look different from the beginning and why?
10. How does the story compare to what you thought it was about when you first saw the cover?

SHARED READING ▶

Extract 1

- Display an enlarged copy of Extract 1. Read the extract aloud and ask: *How are the grandparents feeling? Which words show you this?* The children should identify anger as the emotion and words such as 'angrily', 'nasty', 'dreadful'. The repeated words 'Never, never' also show their annoyance.

- Next, circle the words 'disturb', 'nasty' and 'dreadful'. Explain each word in everyday language and model how you would use them in sentences.

- Tell the children you are going to play a game called 'Three things'. In this game, each child must think of three things that:

    - can disturb (a loud noise, a person interrupting, an alarm)
    - are nasty (tastes, behaviour, smells)
    - can be described as dreadful (a monster, an accident, how you feel when you're ill).

- Challenge them to think of ideas that they don't think anyone else will say.

Extract 2

- Read Extract 2 with the children and ask them why '…Bill and Janet!' is in larger lettering than the rest of the words on the page. (It reveals the answer to the cliffhanger on the previous spread and shows the Smeds' and the Smoos' excitement at finding the pair.)

- Circle the three successive words: 'joy', 'jam' and 'jumping' and ask what they all have in common (they all begin with the letter 'j'). Explain that this is a technique called alliteration and authors use this to create a special effect or mood. Explore together what mood the words create here (happiness, joy, excitement).

- Read aloud the last paragraph on the spread twice – at first, read it in a boring monotone and the next time, excitedly. Ask: *Which version did you like the best?* Hopefully, they will prefer the second! Put the children into pairs and ask them to have a go at saying the words so they can hear the difference between reading aloud with feeling and putting no emotion into their expression.

Extract 3

- Display an enlarged copy of Extract 3 and explain that this extract is non-fiction as it discusses the topic of nonsense poems. Look at the words in the 'Useful words' box, explaining any that are new to the children. Point out that they match the bold words in the text to help the reader.

- Ask the children if they know what a nonsense poem is. (It is a poem that includes funny, made-up words or tells strange, impossible stories.) If possible, have a few nonsense poems to hand to share with the children.

- Read the two verses from 'Jabberwocky' with a lot of drama!

- Next, ask the children if they can give you examples of nonsense words from the verses. Circle their answers. Ask: *Do you think the words work well in the poem?*

- Ask the children if they can guess what the words mean, while reassuring them that there isn't necessarily a right or wrong answer. See if they can substitute the nonsense words with real ones and ask if the poem sounds as effective with real, instead of nonsense, words.

Extract 1

...Till who should disturb them
but Grandfather Smed,
Shaking his fist as he angrily said:

"Never, never play with a Smoo.
They're such a nasty shade of blue.
For the hundredth time I say to you,
Never, never play with a Smoo."

Grandmother Smoo was close behind
And this is how she spoke her mind:

"Never, never play with a Smed.
They're such a dreadful shade of red.
I'll say again what I've always said:
Never, never play with a Smed."

Extract 2

...Bill and Janet!

The rocket touched down, and they ran to the wood
Where the trockles grew tall and the glompoms
smelled good.
And there in a glade, by the rocket of red,
Were the runaway Smoo and the runaway Smed.
(They'd got lost and flown home again, only to find
That all of the others had left them behind.)

There was joy, jam and jumping. Then Janet said, "Maybe
You'd like to make friends with our dear little baby?"
A baby! A red one? A blue one? But no–

Extract 3

Nonsense poems

A nonsense poem has real words mixed up with imaginary ones. There are some of these words in *The Smeds and The Smoos*. Can you think of any?

One of the most famous nonsense poems is 'Jabberwocky' by Lewis Carroll, who also wrote *Alice's Adventures in Wonderland*. Look at these verses:

"Beware the Jabberwock, my son!
The jaws that bite, the claws that catch!
Beware the Jubjub bird, and shun
The frumious Bandersnatch!"

...

And, as in uffish thought he stood,
The Jabberwock, with eyes of flame,
Came whiffling through the tulgey wood,
And burbled as it came!

For nonsense poems to work well, the reader must always be able to understand most of the words. If it was all nonsense, it wouldn't be funny because no one would know what it was about!

Useful words

imaginary

famous

verses

beware

shun

burbled

PHONICS & SPELLING

1. One or more?

Objective
To use the spelling rule for adding '-s' or '-es' as the plural marker for nouns.

What you need
Copies of *The Smeds and The Smoos.*

What to do

- Recall together the rule for making noun endings plural. (If the plural ending sounds like 's' or 'z', then write an 's' at the end of the word. If it sounds like 'iz', then add 'es'.) Provide a few examples of each to ensure children understand ('toys', 'cars', 'watches', 'buses').

- Next, write up on the board the following nouns from the book: 'planet', 'rocket', 'night', 'morning'. Read each one aloud and ask the children how you should make them plural (add an 's' to the end).

- Then, write up the words 'trockle', 'squoon', 'Smed', 'Smoo' and read each one of those aloud. Ask how to make *these* words plural. Explain that even though they are nonsense words, the same rules apply for making them plural as for real words – you just add an 's' to them.

- Write on the board 'wish', 'fox', 'coach'. Say each of the words together aloud, underlining the word endings ('x', 'sh' and 'ch'). Then, say their plurals aloud together, listening for the 'iz' sound, and ask the children how to spell them (you add 'es': 'wishes', 'foxes', 'coaches').

- Finally, ask pairs to write the plurals for 'stew', 'box', 'lake', 'fist' and 'dish'.

Differentiation
Extension: Challenge children to find plurals ending in 's' in the story and write their singular nouns ('holes' – 'hole', 'kangaroos' – 'kangaroo', 'grandparents' – 'grandparent' and so on).

2. Shorter and longer

Objective
To read words with contractions and understand that the apostrophe represents the omitted letter(s).

What you need
Copies of *The Smeds and the Smoos*

What to do

- Start with a reminder of what a contraction is: the bringing together of two words to make one by leaving out one or more letters and adding an apostrophe. Write on the board: 'they're such a nasty shade of blue,' and 'they didn't find Bill'. Circle the contractions and talk about the words that have been shortened ('they're' = 'they are'; 'didn't' = 'did not').

- Explain that we use contractions when we speak because they are shorter and easier to say. Say: *It's fun going to the beach, but it isn't when the weather's bad.* Then, write it on the board and ask the children to identify the contractions ('It's' = 'It is'; 'isn't' = 'is not'; 'weather's' = 'weather is').

- Read aloud this passage from the book, first with the contraction ('they're') and next without it ('they are'). Really emphasise 'they are' in its full form: 'Never, never marry a Smoo./They're a beastly bunch!/They're a crazy crew!'

- Ask the children if they notice a difference to the rhythm. (The contracted version flows more easily and naturally; the full version sounds stilted and formal.)

- Finally, write on the board all the contractions from the book ('They're', 'I'll', 'I've', 'It's', 'who's', 'didn't', 'they'd', 'You'd'). Ask the children to change the contractions back to their full form.

3. Have you ever?

Objective
To use relevant strategies to build their vocabulary.

What you need
Copies of *The Smeds and The Smoos*, a dictionary.

What to do

- First, write the words 'crept', 'decided' and 'beastly' on the board.

- Next, explain that you are going to read a couple of pages aloud from *The Smeds and The Smoos*, where Janet and Bill keep meeting up despite their grandparents' orders not to (spread 6). Instruct the children to listen out for the three words on the board.

- Once you have read the passage aloud, return to the vocabulary and provide the children with a definition for each word, putting them into a sentence that is different to the one used in the story. Use everyday language. For example, say: *The word 'crept' means that Janet and Bill moved very carefully and quietly so that no one could hear or see them; 'decided' means to choose to do or say something. Bill and Janet decided to get married, so this means they thought about it and chose to do it; the word 'beastly' means that something is really unpleasant or nasty. Like a beast!*

- Next, share a definition of each word from a dictionary to consolidate their understanding.

- Once you feel confident that the children understand the meanings of the words, tell them you are going to play a game called 'Have You Ever…?'. Write the following questions on the board for pairs to discuss: 1. 'Have you ever crept somewhere?', 'Why did you move like this?' 2. 'Have you ever decided to do or say something?', 'What was it?' 3. 'Have you ever thought someone or even something was 'beastly'?'. Remind the children to use the focus words in their discussions.

- Bring the class together to share answers.

4. Present, past

Objective
To use '-ed' where no change is needed in the spelling of root words.

What you need
Copies of *The Smeds and The Smoos*, individual whiteboards.

What to do

- Explain that you are going to look at how to spell words in the past tense.

- First, ask the children if they know what a suffix is (an ending that you add to the root of a word).

- Next, ask if they can remember how to put a verb into the past tense. (You usually add 'ed' to the root word if it ends in two consonants or if the word ends in a vowel and a consonant).

- As an example, write the following sentence from the book on the board: 'The Smoos jumped about on their humplety hill.' Underline the word 'jumped' and explain that 'jump' is the present tense of the verb and 'jumped' is the past tense. Model a few examples orally, for example, 'touch' becomes 'touched', 'swallow' becomes 'swallowed'.

- When you think that the children are more confident with this rule, write a few verbs on the board (for example, 'allow', 'crack', 'lock'). Ask for volunteers to come up and change the root word into the past tense ('allow' becomes 'allowed' and so on).

- Tell the children that you are going to write some verbs from *The Smeds and The Smoos* on the board. They should write each one on their whiteboards in the past tense, using the '-ed' suffix. (Example words could include: 'play', 'miss', 'smell', 'clamber', 'disappear', 'press', 'climb', 'reach', 'search', 'splash'.)

- When they have finished, ask the children to swap their whiteboards with a partner and mark the answers together.

Differentiation
Extension: Children write short sentences which include the words they have written.

PLOT, CHARACTER & SETTING ▶

1. Signs of friendship

> **Objective**
> To link what they read or hear read to their own experiences.
>
> **What you need**
> Copies of *The Smeds and The Smoos*.
>
> **Cross-curricular link**
> PSHE

What to do

- Re-read the spread in the book where Janet and Bill meet in the Wurpular Wood (spread 4).

- Ask: *Why do you think Janet and Bill left their usual friends?* (They were bored – see spread 3; perhaps they wanted to meet someone different from themselves for a change.) Ask: *How do you think Janet and Bill feel when they first see each other?*

- Ask: *Why do Janet and Bill rub antennae when they meet?* Answers could include that it's their way of shaking hands or another type of greeting between friends. *How else do they show friendship towards each other?* (Janet tells Bill a story and he sings her a song.)

- Next, ask the children to think about any other signs of friendship that they see in the book, particularly towards the end. Ask them to find and discuss them together. (The Smeds share their pink milk with the Smoos; Grandmother Smoo cuts Grandfather Smed's hair; they all hug the Smoo-Smed; Grandpa and Gran hug each other; they all dance and splash and laugh; they make the baby toys to play with and give him juice from the jerberrycoot; they sing together.)

- Finally, ask the children what signs of friendship they have shown to others, or have had shown to them. You could give some suggestions from your own experience.

2. From start to finish

> **Objective**
> To discuss the sequence of events.
>
> **What you need**
> Copies of *The Smeds and The Smoos*.

What to do

- Before the lesson begins, write the following sentences on the board, in a jumbled-up order: 'The Smeds and the Smoos aren't friends.'; 'Janet and Bill become friends.'; 'One day they run away together in the Smeds' rocket.'; 'The Smeds and the Smoos try to find them.'; 'Janet and Bill are at home with their baby.'; 'Everyone is friends.'

- Explain to the children that stories usually follow a specific order of events so that the narrative makes sense as it progresses from start to finish.

- Ask volunteers to retell the story of a book that you have either read together as a class or one that they have read in their own time. You could start this off by retelling one that you know they are familiar with and highlighting the main sequence of events.

- Explain that you are going to re-read *The Smeds and The Smoos* together and that you want them to pay special attention to the order in which events happen in the book.

- Once you have finished reading the story aloud, divide the children into pairs or small groups. Tell them that you have written the main events of the book on the board but not in order. Ask them to work together to decide the correct order of events and note down the sequence.

- Bring the class together to share answers.

3. The jellyful jerberrycoot

Objective

To participate in discussion about what is read to them, taking turns and listening to what others say.

What you need

Copies of *The Smeds and The Smoos.*

What to do

- Together, read the spread where Janet and Bill meet for the first time in the Wurpular Wood (spread 4). Repeat the lines: 'Then they climbed to the top of a jerberrycoot/And nibbled its juicy and jellyful fruit'.

- Next, encourage the children to think about any food they have eaten recently and to discuss adjectives describing how the food tasted, for example: 'sweet', 'sour', 'spicy', 'salty', 'juicy', 'peppery', 'bitter' and so on. Suggest foods to think about, if necessary. Write their adjectives on the board.

- With these adjectives in mind, encourage the children to suggest what the word 'jellyful' might mean and what the jerberrycoot fruit tastes like from the description and the image on the page. Ask: *Is it sweet? Is it sour? Does it taste like jelly? Does it taste like any other fruit you have tasted?* Remind the children that this is a nonsense book so even though it is 'juicy', it might not taste as we might expect!

- Ask the children what other food and drink is mentioned in the book. (The Smoos drink black tea and eat green stew, while the Smeds drink pink milk and eat brown bread.) Write these on the board.

- Then, ask small groups to discuss what these items might taste like. (The black tea might be a little bitter, for example, while some children might think of pink milk as tasting like strawberry milk, so it could be sweet.) Remind them to use the adjectives on the board, to take turns in speaking and to listen to each other's suggestions.

- Bring the class back together to share ideas.

4. All in a name?

Objective

To make inferences on the basis of what is being said and done.

What you need

Copies of *The Smeds and The Smoos.*

Cross-curricular links

PSHE, art and design

What to do

- 'Smeds' and 'Smoos' are strange and unusual names! However, there is some sense to them: 'Smed' rhymes with 'red', which is the colour of the Smeds, and 'Smoo' rhymes with 'blue', which is the colour of the Smoos. Point out also that the beginning of their names is the same ('Sm'). Ask: *Do you think that aliens should always have strange names? Why/why not?*

- 'Janet' and 'Bill' are everyday names in comparison to the other names in the book. Ask the children why they have been given these rather than something more unusual. (Perhaps to show that they are just 'normal' in their outlook towards each other – they accept each other for who they are rather than seeing each other as 'aliens'.)

- List all the names of the different groups featured in the book on the board: 'Smeds', 'Smoos', 'Vums', 'Scloopies' and 'Klabs'. Ask the children what they think of the names. *Do they sound nice? Are they funny? Why give names like this to creatures who we assume are aliens?* (Answers could include: the names are amusing; they sound strange – like aliens; they are not like words we encounter in English – like a different language.)

- Ask the children to draw a picture of their own alien and give it a name.

- When they have finished, ask the children to present their aliens to the class, describing the different features and colours. Encourage them to explain how they created the name for their creature. (You may want to keep their work from Activity 5 'A load of nonsense!')

Differentiation

Extension: Children make up a story (orally) about their alien meeting another alien from the class.

5. A load of nonsense!

Objective
To listen to and discuss a wide range of poems at a level beyond that at which they can read independently.

What you need
Copies of *The Smeds and The Smoos*, Extract 3, photocopiable page 20 'A load of nonsense!', other nonsense poems to share, such as 'The Owl and the Pussycat', or any poems for children by Edward Lear or Spike Milligan.

What to do
- Ask the children to recall what a nonsense poem is from their work on Extract 3 (poems that use made-up words to make the readers laugh or to create certain sounds). Read them the extract from 'Jabberwocky' again, plus any other nonsense poems you have found. Discuss nonsense words and phrases together and write examples on the board.

- Then, read the first line of the last spread of *The Smeds and The Smoos*: 'Then they sang by the light of the silvery squoon'. Ask: *What do you think* 'squoon' *means here?* (the planet that's like a strange-shaped moon in the picture) *Why?* (The word sounds like 'moon' and the description around it – 'silvery' in terms of light – helps us give meaning to a nonsense word. Explain that this is how nonsense poems make sense.)

- Hand out photocopiable page 20 'A load of nonsense'. Explain to the children that they are going to write a nonsense poem about their own alien. To help get them started, they answer the questions about their alien and draw them (if appropriate they could develop their idea from Activity 4 'All in a name?') before writing their poem on a separate sheet. Encourage them to experiment with words, using the ideas on the board and remembering funny language from *The Smeds and The Smoos*.

- Share alien pictures and poems as a class.

Differentiation
Support: Children draw their alien and write notes.

6. Plan a planet

Objective
To articulate and justify answers, arguments and opinions.

What you need
Copies of *The Smeds and The Smoos*, internet access, photocopiable page 21 'Plan a planet'.

Cross-curricular links
Geography, science, art and design

What to do
- Remind the children that in *The Smeds and The Smoos* the characters travel to all sorts of different planets to look for Janet and Bill. Show them the spreads of the planets of Vumjum, Lurglestrop, Grimbletosh, Glurch, Scloop and Kabloo, and ask them to describe what they see for each one. For example: 'Vumjum looks like a desert'; 'Lurglestrop is pretty and flowery'; 'Grimbletosh looks dirty and smoky'; 'Glurch is damp, wet and gooey'.

- Ask the children if they think the names suit the places and if they can add their own descriptions and observations.

- Strangely, the author doesn't give the Smeds' and the Smoos' planet a name. Ask: *Can you think of a good one?*

- Tell the children that they are going to draw a pictorial map of the planet where the Smeds and the Smoos live. To help them visualise what a map like this should look like, do an internet search for 'maps of the Hundred Acre Wood' and 'maps of Never Never Land' and display them.

- Next, hand out photocopiable page 21 'Plan a planet'. Tell the children that when they are planning their map, they should remember to include such places as the loobular lake, the Wurpular Wood and the humplety hill. They should also refer to the book to help them get an idea of the sort of features on the landscape.

- Ask the children to share their maps and explain how they decided on their planet name.

Differentiation
Support: Children draw a picture of where the Smeds/Smoos live.

 # A load of nonsense!

• Write notes about your alien and draw a picture of them.

What is your alien's name? _____

_____

Describe where they live: _____

_____

_____

What are they like? (small or large, shape, colour, hair, eyes)

_____

_____

What do they like to do?

_____

_____

_____

_____

_____

_____

_____

Plan a planet

- Think of a name for the planet where the Smeds and the Smoos live.
- Draw a map of the planet.

TALK ABOUT IT ▶

1. Suspicious and scowling

Objective
To listen and respond appropriately to adults and peers.

What you need
Copies of *The Smeds and The Smoos*.

What to do

• Re-read the spread in the book where the Smeds and the Smoos discover that Janet and Bill are missing and ask: *How do you think they feel?* (worried, frightened, puzzled, panicked) Encourage the children to look at the illustrations, too, especially the facial expressions.

• Next, focus on the accusations the Smeds and the Smoos make and write on the board: 'stolen', 'taken', 'lured', 'suspicious', 'scowling'. Ask if the children know what these words mean or if they can guess according to their context and the illustrations ('stolen' and 'lured' mean that they believe either Janet or Bill tried to take the other away against their will; 'suspicious' means they don't trust each other).

• Write on the board: 'Smeds: 'Your Bill must have stolen our Janet/And taken her off to a distant planet.''; 'Smoos: 'It's Janet who's stolen our Bill/And lured him away from the humplety hill.''

• Split the class in half – one half are Smeds and the other half are Smoos. Ask them to practise saying their line from the board.

• Then, call the class back and count them in to chorally say their lines, with the Smeds going first. Swap lines and repeat.

• Finally, ask: *Have you ever been in a similar situation, where you were angry with someone and then ended up helping each other?* Encourage children to share their experiences.

2. Say and show

Objective
To give well-structured descriptions, explanations and narratives for different purposes.

What you need
Copies of *The Smeds and The Smoos*, individual whiteboards.

Cross-curricular links
Drama, PE

What to do

• Begin the lesson by asking the children if they can recall what a verb is and if they can give examples.

• Explain that a well-chosen verb can describe how a character is doing an action. Write the verb 'to walk' on the board and explain that you can use other verbs that describe more effectively *how* someone is walking ('march' and 'stride' mean walking with a lot of energy, whereas 'stroll' is a slower walk). Model how the actions would work for these and ask the children to copy you.

• Next, explain that there are many different descriptive verbs in *The Smeds and The Smoos* to tell the reader how a character is moving. Write on the board: 'tiptoe', 'climb', 'nibble', 'creep', 'clamber', 'scowl', 'wave', 'dance'. Define any unfamiliar words. Say them aloud, pausing after each one to ask the children to perform the relevant action.

• Ask pairs to write simple sentences that include each of the verbs on the board.

• Bring the class back together to share their sentences.

Differentiation
Support: Provide sentence openers, such as 'Janet and Bill climb up…'; 'We clamber over…', to help children get started.

Extension: Children present their sentences with actions.

3. If I were a Smoo...

Objective
To participate in role play and improvisations.

What you need
Copies of *The Smeds and The Smoos*.

Cross-curricular link
PSHE

What to do

- Tell the children that you are going to re-read *The Smeds and The Smoos* and, this time, you want them to think about Janet and Bill's friendship throughout the story.

- After you have finished reading the book, ask: *Do you think Janet and Bill were different to the other Smeds and Smoos? Why did they ignore what they were told and meet up with each other?* Write the children's suggestions on the board (for example, they liked each other and wanted to be friends).

- Next, split the children into pairs and ask them to each choose to be the character of either Janet or Bill. Explain that they are going to be asked about their character's experiences in the story. Write these questions on the board: Why did you disobey your family?; Why do you like each other?; Was it scary going against everyone else to be friends?; Where did you go in the Smeds' red rocket?; How did you feel when you came back and everyone else had left?; What will happen in the future for the Smeds and the Smoos?

- Ask pairs to practise asking each other these questions, answering as their character, thinking about how their character would feel. Point out that the story does not answer the questions and so they will need to use their imagination and give their own ideas.

- Bring the class back together. Ask for volunteers to talk as Janet or Bill about why they chose to be friends and what happened.

Differentiation
Support: Discuss the questions and explore possible answers as a class before splitting children into pairs.

4. Friends forever

Objective
To consider and evaluate different viewpoints, attending to and building on the contributions of others.

What you need
Copies of *The Smeds and The Smoos*, photocopiable page 25 'Friends forever', art materials.

Cross-curricular links
PSHE, art and design

What to do

- Explain to the children that one of the main themes of the book is friendship and how people decide who to be friends with. Ask: *How do the Smeds and the Smoos feel about each other at the beginning of the book?* (They are suspicious of and dislike each other.) *Explain why you think they feel this way.* (Answers could include the Smeds and the Smoos look different from each other, like different things and behave differently.)

- Ask the children if these are good reasons to decide whether to be friends with someone or not. Discuss their ideas together sensitively and explore how the Smeds and the Smoos change their minds during the story.

- Next, discuss what a good friend is like. Ask: *What adjectives could you use?* (For example: 'kind', 'helpful', 'fun', 'funny', 'caring'.) Write these on the board and perhaps include some new ones, such as 'warm', 'loving', 'brave'. Encourage the children to listen to different viewpoints and remind them that not everyone wants exactly the same things in a friend.

- Hand out photocopiable page 25 'Friends forever' and read it together. Tell the children that you want them to draw a picture of one of their friends (or someone they like). Below their drawing they should write the adjectives that they feel best describe the person.

- When the children have finished, ask them to share their pictures with the class.

Differentiation
Extension: Children write simple sentences about their friends, using capital letters and full stops.

5. Mark my reading!

Objective
To speak audibly and fluently.

What you need
Copies of *The Smeds and The Smoos*, individual whiteboards.

Cross-curricular link
Drama

What to do

- Explain to the children that part of reading aloud well involves using expression. Discuss together what expression means: using different tones of voice, speaking louder or more quietly, putting emotion into the words, speeding up and slowing down. Ask: *Why is it good to use expression?* (It adds interest to the words; it makes the story more exciting, scary or funny.)

- Next, explain that you are going to read aloud a passage from *The Smeds and The Smoos* and you want them to give you a score out of 5 for how well you read it (5 being the highest). They must be honest!

- Read out any extract where either Grandfather Smed or Grandmother Smoo is telling off their grandchild about mixing with 'the enemy'. The first time you read it, put a lot of expression and intonation into your voice – don't be afraid to exaggerate. When you have finished, ask the children to show you their scores for your performance (hopefully they will have scored you 4 or 5).

- Next, read out the same passage but do so in the most boring voice you can manage: a slow monotone, if possible, with no emphasis or expression. Ask the children to score you on this (hopefully, you should score no more than 1 or 2).

- Then, ask pairs to practise performing the same extract from the book, experimenting with expression and making sure their speech flows.

- Ask volunteers to perform their piece in front of the class.

Differentiation
Extension: Children perform another extract where the grandparents tell off Janet and Bill.

6. Qs and As

Objective
To ask relevant questions to extend their understanding and knowledge.

What you need
Copies of *The Smeds and The Smoos*, internet access to written or recorded interviews with children's authors and with Julia Donaldson and/or Axel Scheffler.

Cross-curricular link
PSHE

What to do

- Start the lesson by asking the children if they can remember what an author and an illustrator do when they are making books. You might need to refresh their knowledge if they aren't sure.

- Tell the children that they are going to think of questions to ask Julia Donaldson, the author, and Axel Scheffler, the illustrator, about *The Smeds and The Smoos*. Play or show any interviews with authors and illustrators of books the children have read so they get an idea of what happens in an interview.

- Ask pairs or small groups to discuss the kinds of question they might like to ask Julia Donaldson and Axel Scheffler. Explain that they should ask questions that are relevant to the book.

- Call the class back together and ask for examples of questions. Write them on the board. For example: 'How did you get the idea for the book?'; 'How did you choose the names for the characters?'; 'Is it difficult to write a book that rhymes?'; 'How did you know how to draw a Smed or a Smoo?'; 'How do you both work together on a book?'

- Role play the interview, with you or the children taking on the role of Julia Donaldson and/or Axel Scheffler. Then, if available, play any interviews of the author and illustrator (ideally talking about *The Smeds and The Smoos*) to see if the children's questions are answered.

Differentiation
Extension: Children think of questions about other books the pair have collaborated on.

Friends forever

- Draw a picture of a friend.

- Write some adjectives to describe what is good about your friend.

_____

_____

_____

_____

GET WRITING ▶

1. Lost!

> ### Objective
> To discuss what they have written with the teacher or other pupils.
>
> ### What you need
> Copies of *The Smeds and The Smoos*.
>
> ### Cross-curricular link
> PSHE

What to do

- At the start of the lesson, remind the children that we never find out where Janet and Bill went when they took the Smeds' rocket. The only information we are told is that 'They'd got lost and flown home again'.

- Tell the children that you want them to imagine what happened to Janet and Bill on their journey. Write the following questions on the board: 'How long were they gone for?'; 'Where did they travel to?'; 'What did they eat?'; 'Did they meet any other creatures? Who?'; 'Did they miss their friends and families?'; 'Were they worried about coming home again in case they were in trouble?'.

- Explain that they should also think about how Janet and Bill felt when they arrived home, only to find everyone else had left.

- Next, divide the children into pairs and ask them to write the answers to some or all of the questions. Ask them to write their answers as sentences. Provide sentence starters on the board to help them if necessary ('We were gone for…'; 'We met…').

- Bring the class back together to discuss their different answers.

> ### Differentiation
> **Support:** Ask children to focus on just one of the questions.
>
> **Extension:** Children write this as a short story, making the ideas flow into a narrative.

2. Smoodles of mistakes!

> ### Objective
> To begin to punctuate sentences using a capital letter and a full stop, question mark or exclamation mark.
>
> ### What you need
> Individual whiteboards

What to do

- Explain that you are going to look at how to write proper sentences. Ask: *How do you begin a sentence?* (You use a capital letter.)

- Next, ask the children for the three different punctuation marks that can end a sentence. Write the punctuation marks on the board and label them. Discuss together when you would use each one. (A full stop is for normal sentences. A question mark is for asking questions. These often begin with words such as 'who', 'what', 'when', 'where', 'why', 'how' and 'do'. An exclamation mark is used at the end of sentences that show strong emotion such as surprise, excitement, happiness, anger and fear.)

- Next, write the following sentences on the board (with no punctuation): 'janet and Bill are good friends'; 'why do the Smeds and the Smoos not like each other'; 'the Wurpular Wood sounds like a fun place to play in'; 'bill and Janet have gone missing – help'; 'back at home, the new baby was very happy'.

- Ask the children to write these sentences, remembering to start with capital letters and end with the correct punctuation.

- When they have finished, go through the answers together.

> ### Differentiation
> **Extension:** Children write some of their own sentences about *The Smeds and The Smoos* using the correct punctuation and capital letters.

3. Order! Order!

Objective
To sequence sentences to form short narratives.

What you need
Copies of *The Smeds and The Smoos,* individual whiteboards.

What to do

- Tell the children that there are three things a story needs for it to make sense: a beginning, a middle and an end. To consolidate, recap the beginning, middle and end of a story you've read recently as a class.

- Ask for volunteers to tell you, in a sentence or two, what happens in the beginning, middle and end of *The Smeds and The Smoos*. Write their answers on the board under the three headings.

- Explain that recipes and instructions also need a beginning, a middle and an end in order to make sense. They have to follow a certain order so that the person reading them knows how to do something.

- Next, put the children into small groups. Explain that you are going to write up a recipe for pink milk on the board, but the steps will not be in the correct order. Their job is to decide on the correct order of the jumbled-up steps and write them down in the correct order on their whiteboards. Write the steps on the board as follows:

  - Drink the pink milk with a straw!
  - Put the milk into a jug.
  - Milk the Smed cow.
  - Pour the milk into a glass.
  - Add pink drops to the milk.

- Make sure the children know all the vocabulary and explain any gaps in knowledge before they start the activity. (Point out that the Smed cow isn't mentioned in the story but is here for the purpose of the activity.)

- Bring the class together to check their answers.

Differentiation
Extension: Children invent recipes for green stew or black tea, focusing on the sequence of the steps.

4. Talented travel agents

Objective
To read aloud their writing clearly enough to be heard by their peers and the teacher.

What you need
Copies of *The Smeds and The Smoos*, art materials, examples of travel adverts from magazines or newspapers.

Cross-curricular link
Art and design

What to do

- Ask the children if they know what a travel agent is (someone who helps people choose holidays and books flights and accommodation). Display some examples of travel adverts and discuss their features together, writing the following headings on the board: 'the main things to do'; 'special food and drink'; 'where to stay/sleep'; and 'how to travel there'.

- Explain that the children are going to plan a holiday poster about the planet where the Smeds and the Smoos live. (They should give the planet a name if they haven't already done so – see page 24 'Plan a Planet' activity in Plot, character and setting.) Discuss the sort of information that could go on this poster and write their ideas under the respective headings on the board. (For example, climbing the trockles in the Wurpular Wood, bouncing on the humplety hill, and swimming in the loobular lake; pink milk, black tea, green stew, brown bread, the fruit of a jerberrycoot tree; in beds or, if they prefer something different, in holes; in a rocket or an imaginary way!)

- Tell the children that they should write short sentences about anything they want to include on their poster and draw interesting, colourful pictures of their chosen information.

- Bring the class together and invite volunteers to try to 'sell' a holiday to their peers via persuasive talk and showing their classmates their posters. Remind them to speak clearly so that everyone can hear.

Differentiation
Support: Children draw and write about one aspect.

Extension: Children write a longer piece of narrative, interspersed with fewer pictures.

5. Trockles and trees

Objective
To say out loud what they are going to write about.

What you need
Copies of *The Smeds and The Smoos*, photocopiable page 29 'Trockles and trees', art materials.

Cross-curricular link
Art and design

What to do
- Show the children the spread in the book where Janet and Bill meet for the first time in the Wurpular Wood (spread 4). Highlight the word 'trockles', which we can assume to be the name of the trees that grow there ('the trockles grew tall').

- Re-read the book together, focusing on the illustrations of trees and plants throughout the story. Discuss with the children the words and sentences they could use to describe the colours and shapes of the trees and plants, and where they are found. (For example, in spread 1 there is a tall, yellow and orange tree by the loobular lake with leaves like fingers; in spread 3 there are plants that look like purple carrots with pointy tops; in spread 4 the trees in the Wurpular Wood look more like our forest trees but the bark is purple and there are strange flowers with spikes growing out of them.)

- Next, explain that the children are going to choose their favourite plant or tree in the story and write a description of it. They can give it a name too, if it's not already named.

- Put the children into pairs and hand out photocopiable page 29 'Trockles and trees' and read it together. Ask the children to discuss with each other which plant or tree they have chosen, what its name is and how they are going to describe it. Then, ask them to work on their sheets individually and encourage them to write complete sentences.

- Bring the class together to share their work.

6. A loobular calendar

Objective
To spell the days of the week.

What you need
Copies of *The Smeds and The Smoos*, photocopiable page 30 'A loobular calendar'.

What to do
- Write the days of the week on the board, starting with Monday. Then, read aloud *The Smeds and The Smoos* from the point where the Smeds and the Smoos set off in the rocket to search for Janet and Bill to when they return to their own planet.

- When you have finished, point out that the Smeds and the Smoos have visited six different planets.

- Hand out photocopiable page 30 'A loobular calendar' to the children. Explain to them that the Smeds and the Smoos want to return to all the planets they visited while looking for Janet and Bill, so they can tell the aliens that all is well. Luckily, they have a brand-new, super-speedy rocket that can do all of this in a week!

- However, the Smeds and the Smoos are having trouble filling in the calendar and need the children's help. In the first gap in each sentence, they should write the correct day of the week. In the second, they should write in the correct name of each planet. For the last day, they can either write the word 'home' or use an invented name for the home planet.

- Explain that they should use the spellings of the days of the week on the board to help them, and that the planets should be written in the order they appear in the book. They can refer to the book and work in pairs.

- When the children have finished, go through the answers together (Monday/Vumjum, Tuesday/Lurglestrop, Wednesday/Grimbletosh, Thursday/Glurch, Friday/Scloop, Saturday/Klaboo, Sunday/home or planet name).

Differentiation
Support: Add the planet names to the sheet so that children only write the days.

Trockles and trees

- Choose your favourite tree or plant in the story and complete the sheet.

My favourite tree/plant is called _____

_____

My picture of it:

How I describe it: _____

_____

_____

_____

A loobular calendar

In the sentences below, fill in the day of the week and the name of the planet the Smeds and the Smoos will visit.

On _____ we'll visit Planet _____, which is coated in grime.

On _____ we'll visit Planet _____, which is covered in roses.

On _____ we'll return to _____.

On _____ we'll visit Planet _____, which is dusty and dry.

On _____ we'll visit Planet _____, where the Klabs walk on stilts.

On _____ we'll visit Planet _____, where the Scloopies wear kilts.

On _____ we'll visit Planet _____, which has nothing but slime.

ASSESSMENT ▶

1. Expand and improve

Objective
To learn how to use expanded noun phrases to describe and specify.

What you need
Copies of *The Smeds and The Smoos*, individual whiteboards.

What to do

- Ask the children if they know or can remember what an expanded noun phrase is (a noun with one or more adjectives describing it). Write some examples on the board, progressing from the simplest of phrases to more detailed ones, such as 'a tall tree', 'a tall, green tree', 'a tall, emerald-green pine tree'.

- Next, write the following expanded noun phrases from *The Smeds and The Smoos* on the board: 'a far-off planet', 'a nasty shade of blue', 'a dreadful shade of red', 'a dry, dusty place'.

- Go through these phrases with the children and ask them to suggest ways of changing them into something else (for example, 'a nearby planet', 'a lovely, cool blue'). Children can work in pairs or small groups to think of alternatives. They should write them on their whiteboards and then share them with the class.

- When they have finished, give the children the nonsense expanded noun phrases 'the silvery squoon', 'the loobular lake' and 'the humplety hill'. Encourage them to think of words to use instead of the nonsense words. Have some fun coming up with real or made-up versions together.

Differentiation
Extension: Ask children to change the expanded noun phrases from the beginning of the activity into nonsense ones.

2. Prequels and sequels

Objective
To use spoken language to develop understanding through speculating, hypothesising, imagining and exploring ideas.

What you need
Copies of *The Smeds and The Smoos*, children's books that form part of a series.

What to do

- Begin by asking the children if they know what a 'sequel' is (the next story in a series of books or films). Then, ask them if they know what a 'prequel' is (the story before the one they have read or watched).

- Ask if they can give you any examples of books or films that have sequels or prequels (for example, the *Toy Story* series, *The Gruffalo* and *The Gruffalo's Child*, or other books they may have read). Show them a series of books. (The *Supertato* series by Sue Hendra is a good example to show the children, or the *Hat* series by Jon Klassen.)

- Next, ask small groups to discuss what could happen in a sequel to *The Smeds and The Smoos*. Ask: *Who would be in it? Would there be new characters? How would the Smeds and the Smoos behave towards each other?* Ask the groups to share their thoughts with the class.

- Then, ask the groups to consider the 'prequel'. They could think about how and why the Smeds and the Smoos became enemies. Ask: *Were they always like that? What happened to make them dislike each other?* Again, invite the children to share their thoughts, justifying their ideas with examples.

Differentiation
Extension: Children write their sequels or prequels with words and pictures.

3. Two becomes one

Objective

To develop their understanding of the concepts set out in English Appendix 2 by joining clauses using 'and'.

What you need

Copies of *The Smeds and The Smoos*, lined paper.

What to do

- Tell the children that you are all going to look at how to use the joining word 'and' in sentences. Explain to them that a joining word is also known as a conjunction.

- Next, tell the children that the word 'and' can be used in different ways as a joining word: either to add more information to a simple sentence ('At school we learn about words *and* numbers') or to join together two different phrases or short sentences ('In the morning I eat breakfast *and* then I go to school'). Explain that by joining two shorter sentences to make one longer one, they can make their writing more interesting.

- Next, hand out lined paper and then write these sentences on the board in two columns:

  1. The Smeds are red.   The Smoos are blue.
  2. The Smeds sleep in beds.   The Smoos sleep in holes.
  3. The Smeds have strange hair.   The Smoos have strange shoes.
  4. The Smeds drink pink milk.   The Smoos drink black tea.
  5. The Smeds eat brown bread.   The Smoos eat green stew.

- Tell the children that they are going to join the sentences on the left with the ones on the right using the joining word 'and' to make one complete sentence ('The Smeds are red and the Smoos are blue'). They should do this for each pair.

- When they have finished, check their work.

Differentiation

Extension: Children also use 'but' to join sentences. They make up their own sentences about the Smeds and the Smoos.

4. Review the Smoos

Objective

To develop positive attitudes towards writing by writing for different purposes.

What you need

Copies of *The Smeds and The Smoos*, art materials, examples of book reviews (preferably written by children).

Cross-curricular link

Art and design

What to do

- Begin the lesson by asking and discussing the following questions:
  - *What is the book about?*
  - *Who are the main characters?*
  - *What happens in the story?*
  - *What did you like about the book?*
  - *Is there anything you didn't like?*
  - *What did you learn by reading this book?*
  - *Would you recommend it to other children?*

- Next, tell the children that they are going to write a book review and check to see if they know what this is. Explain that good book reviews talk about everything you've just discussed, and they give an honest opinion about a book. They don't give away the ending though!

- Show the children examples. Read out the reviews and ask the children whether they are helpful or not. Ask: *Have you read any of the books mentioned? Do you agree with the reviews?*

- Next, explain that they are going to write a book review about *The Smeds and The Smoos*, using everything they can remember about the story. They should include the following information: title of book, names of author and illustrator, what the book is about, their opinion, whether they recommend the book or not.

- They could also draw a picture of a scene in the book that they particularly enjoyed.

Differentiation

Support: Children write about their favourite part of the book.